# YOUR KNOWLEDGE HAS VALUE

# The Cultural Industry in Germany. Application of Adornos Theories to "RTL" and its Reality-TV

Lisa Hagen

**Bibliographic information published by the German National Library:**

The German National Library lists this publication in the National Bibliography; detailed bibliographic data are available on the Internet at http://dnb.dnb.de.

ISBN: 9783346830555
This book is also available as an ebook.

© GRIN Publishing GmbH
Nymphenburger Straße 86
80636 München

Print and binding: Books on Demand GmbH, Norderstedt, Germany
Printed on acid-free paper from responsible sources.

The present work has been carefully prepared. Nevertheless, authors and publishers do not incur liability for the correctness of information, notes, links and advice as well as any printing errors.

GRIN web shop: https://www.grin.com/document/1333702

RESEARCH PAPER

# CULTURAL INDUSTRY IN GERMANY APPLICATION OF ADORNOS IDEAS TO „RTL" AND ITS REALITY-TV

Student: Lisa Hagen
Date of Submission: 2018.12.19

# Content

# Introduction

Since the beginning of the 1990s, television entertainment in Germany changed. The audience became more and more actor, especially within private channels. Interpersonal relationships and the daily lives of private individuals are of growing importance in performative terms.[1] Therefore, Reality TV became a relevant genre. Reality TV, often called "Trash TV" is highly embedded in the current television environment and TV shows like "Ich bin ein Star – Holt mich hier raus!" belong to the most popular programs within the country. This papers' purpose is to analyse this genre and find certain patters which help these shows to be successful. Furthermore, this article deals with one of the most known theories in terms of culture industry. The German philosopher and sociologist Adornos advocates a very pessimistic view on this phenomenon which is applied here as vehicle to classify the private channel „RTL" and its program offerings, especially Reality TV. I want to find out if his gloomy ideas became realized there.

## 1. Introduction of Reality-TV

Reality TV is a hybrid genre which merges authenticity with production.[2] As the name implies, it suggests an attempt to portray reality through the medium of television. These programs are made to overcome the scripted nature of television shows and their predetermined endings by 'real people' in 'real situations' which should evoke the feeling of honest. But this "reality" is only partly true. For example, considering "Ich bin ein Star – Holt mich hier raus", nobody finds his- or herself suddenly in the middle of an Australian jungle, forced to play games in order not to starve.[3] Nevertheless, these programs are expected to be perceived as more real than fictitious scripted contents. Especially, because the consumer gets the feeling of

---

[1] Doeveling, Katrin (2008). P.2.
[2] Ibid., P.2.
[3] Potts, Graham (2007). P. 1.

monitoring the daily life rhythm of the characters. That means, that the recipient can see the show-members in almost every daily life situation, like they were part of a panopticon. The participants on the other side of the screen have the certainty that everything they say or do can be taped and thence be watched. In the end, only few parts of the total recorded material are aired, and the distillate is broadcasted in several episodes. Another main characteristic of these shows is the fact, that the displayed personalities aren't professional actors and therefore receiving less money than professionals. Some of the shows' actors are former consumers which realised the possibility of being an active part in their favourite show. This made producers and consumers switching their places. Producers can just let things happen and watch selected participants doing the show. Consequently, the producers accept to lose a part of their control. But they still have a lot of power during the editing process which is invisible to the audience.[4] The production turns into a quasi-social experiment which is characterised by uncertainty. Therefore, the producers try to attract preferably interesting people and make them producing interesting outcomes when they meet each other. The goal is to create drama and conflict. To push this process, they also tend to put their candidates in extreme situations which can include the absence of food or money. The members therefore give away the control over their life conditions. [5] This blurs the line between the reality of their everyday lives and the media world.[6]

Especially, during the last years a strong re-fictionalization is remarkable. This leads to three major effects: Firstly, it creates a merger of reality pretension and reality intervention. Consequently, this staging itself produces reality. This in turn leads to dissolution between leisure time and working time and stardom because the integration of ordinary people in the entertainment program of television is a field of work and its career opportunities. The result is

---

[4] Bleicher, Joan Kristin (2018). Last Access on 2018.12.01.
[5] Mark, Andrejevic (2003). P. 82 - 83.
[6] Doeveling, Katrin (2008). P. 3.

the so called "celebrification". Thirdly, the merger of fact and fiction is a new challenge for its audience to be critic and attentively. [7]

## 2. Reality TV in Germany

In terms of reality TV, the German „RTL" group is a crucial player. Consequently, this broadcaster is a suitable vehicle to approach the phenomenon of Reality TV in this country. Nowadays, „RTL" is one of the most popular television channels there. For September 2018, the TV ratings for the „RTL" group is 28,4% of the 14-59-year olds. The „RTL" group currently operates six free-TV and four Pay-TV channels.[8] Furthermore, it owns several broadcasting rights in the sports field, for example boxing or Formula 1. And then, there is Reality TV like, "Ich bin ein Star – Holt mich hier raus" which is the most popular television content among the young audience, even more popular than sport-events.[9] Reality TV often has to face the designation of "Trash TV". This perception is based on low-quality contents and the perpetually critic which is rest on the fact that these programs perform on the edges of the levels, taste and disgust.[10] The "Stern" magazine published a statistic that shows, that especially „RTL"2 and „RTL" are highly regarded as "Trash-TV" producers.[11] "Stern" furthermore recorded this public opinion in the following statistic where all of the mentioned programs are broadcasted by one of „RTL"s' channels.[12] Though this bad reputation, „RTL" is broadcaster of 9 of the 20 most popular television shows in Germany.[13] Therefore, its impact on the society shouldn't be underestimated.

---

[7] Neumann-Braun, Klaus (n.d.). Last Access 2018.12.01.
[8] Presseportal (2018). Last Access on 2018.11.28.
[9] Grzeschik, David (2018). Last Access on 2018.10.20.
[10] Seier, Andrea (2014). P. 37 – 38.
[11] Stern (2018). Last Access on 2018.12.10.
[12] Stern (2017). Last Access on 2018.12.01.
[13] Welt (n.d.). Last Access on 2018.11.20.

*This image was removed due to copyright reasons.*

*Figure 1:Source: Statista*

The explanation for the strong focus on Reality TV programs is the dual broadcasting system which evolved since the 1980s. Due this development, a competition between the public service broadcasters, like ZDF and the private commercial channels, as „RTL" erupted. 35,7% of the private channel „RTL"s broadcasting time is occupied by non-fictional content in 2011. ZDF in comparison uses 46,9% of its time on air with informational content. This is because ZDF is a public channel which is supported by the government and has therefore to adhere to the program contract of mediate information. Revenues from advertising are playing a secondary role. But especially these kinds of profits are necessary for private channels like „RTL" which leads to high pressure. Consequently, the offered program is highly oriented towards the audiences' interests and entertainment programs including lifelike orientations are the first choice. [14] In the following section this paper introduces certain Reality TV programs broadcasted by „RTL".

---

[14] Stubenböck, Julia (2014). P. 12.

## 2.1. Reality TV Programs based on the Evolvement of Romantic Relationships

"Bauer sucht Frau" is the German adaption of a British format and the 14th season is already on TV.[15] The show primarily addresses emotions since it focuses on the evolvement of relationships between a farmer and the woman he chose at the barn festival in the beginning of the season. The recipients have the chance to empathize with the participants when they reveal their feelings to each other. Besides, the individuals' clumsiness and embarrassing moments are crucial elements of the show which aims for displaying characters who differ from norms through unusual behaviour and appearance, eccentricity and inexperience with women. The participants are platforms for identification on the one side and figures of fun on the other side. Furthermore, the show creates a sense of intimacy through displaying the living sphere of the famers and intimate moments with their chosen one. The audience becomes a voyeur. The last crucial element is the voiceover. What is the presenter for "Ich bin ein Star – Holt mich hier raus" is the commentator for "Bauer sucht Frau". The voiceover puts the setting in a theoretical framework and functions like a (sarcastic) narrator. This judgmental element is a key item for the creation of drama if the visual material isn't enough.[16] In 2018, the average viewing rate of "Bauer sucht Frau" among the 14-49-year-old ones was 1,72 Mio. (18,2 %).[17]

"Bauer sucht Frau" is not the only show which places the focus on romantic issues. In Germany, it seems like every program which has "Bachelor" in its title is going to be successful. "Der Bachelor" has its origin in America and was firstly broadcasted there in 2002. The same happened with "The Bachelorette" which started in America in 2003 and the spin-off "Bachelor in Paradise" which was firstly broadcasted in 2014 there. In Germany, the first season "Der Bachelor" started in 2003, followed by "Die Bachelorette" in 2004. In May 2018, "Bachelor in

---

[15] Chalaby, Jean K. (2011). P. 302.
[16] Lehmann, Sophie (2012). P. 26 - 28.
[17] Sallhoff, Daniel (2017). Last Access on 2018.12.05.

Paradise" was broadcasted for the first time. All these programs are still ongoing. Thereby, the principle is always the same: young and good-looking people are searching for love. In "Der Bachelor", one man chooses between 20 women. Therefore, he gets to know the participants through group- or single-dates at extraordinary places, like beaches or helicopter flights. Every week, he must eliminate one woman by giving her no rose, the hallmark of the show. By being asked "Nimmst du diese Rose an?" ("Do you accept this rose?"), the girl can refuse or agree to continue. If she doesn't take the rose, she decides to leave the show by herself. "Die Bachelorette" operates the other way around. One woman can choose her jack of hearts out of 20 candidates. One interesting fact here is, that "Der Bachelor" wasn't broadcasted during the time from 2004 until 2011. The reason for this break was the failure of "The Bachelorette" in 2004. In 2011 "„RTL"" gave this format another chance.[18] "Der Bachelor" reached up to 20,8% of German television recipients in January 2018, "Bachelorette" up until 18,6% in Juli 2017 and "Bachelor in Paradise" which mixes up 24 candidates from former "Der Bachelor" or "Die Bachelorette" seasons, to find their love there, reached 7,8% in average, which means 2,07 million recipients in absolute value. Among the 14-49-year-old target group the viewing rates reached even 15,5%.[19]

## 2.2. Reality TV Programs based on Surveillance

"Big Brother" was firstly broadcasted in the Netherlands in 1999 and in Germany in 2000 by „RTL". Currently, this program was completely innovative. The participants had to live for more than three months a staged everyday life without any contacts to the outside world. The shows' cast is aware of this artificial situation and the omnipresence of cameras even though the participants tend to forget it temporarily. The members have to carry out a quasi-real daily life which includes every ordinary activity, like brushing teeth or communicate with the

---

[18] Niemeier, Timo (2012). Last Access on 2018.12.07.
[19] Grzeschik, David (2018). Last Access on 2018.12.15.

roommates. The recipient can watch all these activities and compare them to his or her own life. This leads to blurring lines between reality and fiction on the one side and between private and public sphere on the other side.[20]

"Big Brother" includes elements of different genres, like the soap-opera because of the daily broadcasted summaries. Even though the candidates are filmed for 24 hours per day, the audience only watches the summary of 45 minutes. But the consumer can watch supplementary content on the internet which enables him or her to watch the cast round the clock. It also involves game show items since the candidates have to play games. Instead of a physical game master, there is the anonymous "Big Brother" who appears through sound boxes. Thereby, the show follows a participative tournament structure which enables audiences' decision making. Like "Ich bin ein Star – Holt mich hier raus!", the consumer can decide who leaves the container. [21]

In Germany, "Big Brother" was broadcasted until 2011 by „RTLII". After a two years break, it appeared again under the title "Promi Big Brother" which is broadcasted by Sat.1. This marks an approximation with the show "Ich bin ein Star – Holt mich hier raus!" regarding the change towards celebrification. The principle of these two shows is very similar and "Ich bin ein Star – Holt mich hier raus!" can be seen as modified version of „Big Brother", because in both, the celebrities find themselves in an artificial and staged situation where they are observed the whole time and forced to play games. In face of the cast selection, producers choose the most interesting and extreme candidates to create spectacular situations like fights or romances.

"Ich bin ein Star – Holt mich hier raus!", broadcasted by „RTL" since 2004, already went through 16 regular editions. In 2017, it reached 6.49 million viewers during the season.[22] The

---

[20] Mikos, Lothar (2000). P. 164 - 166.
[21] Ibid., P. 171 - 175.
[22] Köpfe (2018). Last Access on 2018.12-09.

basis of this format is "I'm a Celebrity ... Get me out of here!" which was firstly on air in Great Britain in 2002.[23] As in "Big Brother" the participants are filmed, when they are sleeping or showering themselves, etc. Because they are watched the whole time, they are very authentic. In order to earn food, the participants have to win games. If they lose, they only get small meals involving rice and beans. Furthermore, the producers take away the members' cigarettes and coffee to put them under psychological stress. Besides, the show includes two presenters who comment the show in a very ironic way. The difference between "Ich bin ein Star – Holt mich hier raus!" and other reality shows is the fact, that the ten participants get high fees for their appearance which range from 50.000€ to 200.000€ and are depending on status and popularity. Participants who say the popular sentence "Ich bin ein Star – Holt mich hier raus!" gain less money because they break up the experiment earlier.[24]

The ten participants live in the Australian jungle. Their aim is to avoid being voted off by the recipients in front of the screen. The disgusting challenges which involve insects, dirt, etc. started a huge debate on German TV and its quality.[25] The cast must pass challenges to get rewards for their whole group. Therefore, these parts of the program create the most critical moments because the members are confronted with their biggest fears, as wild animals. Like the previous mentioned shows, this program includes competition. Here, the candidates must fight against each other for the most fan-support.[26] Furthermore, the cast usually exposes sensitive information about themselves in front of the campfire which creates the spectacularly character of the show. This is the chance for the recipient to get to know more about the participants.

---

[23] Maeder, Dominik (2018). P. 78.
[24] Zeitungsverlag tz München GmbH & Co. KG (2018). Last Access on 2018.11.06.
[25] Maeder, Dominik (2018). P. 78.
[26] Ibid., P. 85 - 86.

## 2.3. Reality TV and its interconnections

It is remarkable, that current Reality TV programs are highly intertwined with each other and assemble various elements, like exoticism which is a main part of "Der Bachelor". All the seasons play in extraordinary surroundings, like Cape Town in 2012. "Ich bin ein Star – Holt mich hier raus!" also includes this element since the participants are located in the Australian jungle during the show. Besides, the attractivity as well as the curiosity of the cast can be identified as popular pattern for reality programs. Furthermore, pseudo-social-experiments with prominent and ordinary people are the base of several shows, like "Promi Big Brother", "Ich bin ein Star – Holt mich hier raus!", "Bachelor in Paradise", etc. which are accompanied by humorous and ironic moderators.[27] "Das Sommerhaus der Stars" which is broadcasted since 2016 is a result of this mixing process. Within this show seven more or less popular couples live in a mansion which is located outside Germany on closest area. Their daily life is pervaded by challenges which the couples have to pass and the elimination process in the end of every episode.

In conclusion, emotion, surveillance, competition and celebrification transpired as key elements of reality shows. It seems like the times are over, where only individual elements were used to produce a show. As "Wer wird Millionär" the German adaption of the British quiz show "Who wants to be a millionaire" shows this process by increasing the inclusion of different events, like specials, as the "Wer wird Millionär? – Prominenten-Special" in 2018.[28] "Deutschland sucht den Superstar", the German version of the British "Pop Idol", which starts its 16th season in 2019, enhanced the involvement of private moments of the contestants. And in turn, the elimination procedure of this show found its way to other programs like "Ich bin ein Star – Holt mich hier raus!", where the audience can decide or "Der Bachelor" where the protagonist

---

[27] Bleicher, Joan Kristin (2018). Last Access on 2018.12.01.
[28] RTL interactive GmbH (2018). Last Access on 2018.12.12.

chooses his number one girl during the season. All these shows are long game shows in which the candidates compete against each other.[29]

One relatively new element within these shows is nakedness. It wasn't part of them for long time due to the tabooing through the society. Shows like "Naked Attraction – Dating hautnah" since 2017 on ",RTLII" or "Adam sucht Eva" since 2014 on ",RTL" use this provocative component to give new allures to their audience. This increases the already considerable voyeuristic character of these shows. "Adam sucht Eva" also started with a cast which consisted of ordinary people. But after two seasons, the producers decided to extend the cast with celebrities. In 2018, the show reached 13,7% of the 14-49-year-olds in average.[30] Besides, all these formats include the motive of seclusion. The candidates are not allowed to contact the external world. It became clear that it's difficult to assign the shows to certain categories. Key characteristics of the audience on the other side, are voyeurism and affair-expectation. They act like external monitors with their indiscreet gaze. This enables a reception in several ways. The individual can decide by itself it becomes a fan of the cast members or a critic.[31]

## 3. Discussion – Are Adorno's Dystopian Ideas realized in ",RTL"?

A key person in this paper is Theodor Wiesengrund Adorno who was part of the Frankfurt school. Adornos ideas are characterised by pessimism. The author opposes the blind belief in progress and enlightenment. According to Adorno and Horkheimer, culture industry is a vehicle of social control which tends to be "ever the same", to a recurring self-similarity and conformity. What counts are technological standards: what is sold to millions of consumers is due to these same consumers and their demands. Art is produced for the consumption of the mass and the only purpose of cultural products is creating profits. Therefore, culture became reduced to

---

[29] Brown, Patrick (2010). Last Access on 2018.12.10.
[30] Nöthling, Timo (2018). Last Access on 2018.12.08.
[31] Meier, Urs (2000). Last Access on 2018.11.20.

entertainment. Culture industry overall has a totalizing tendency and the commercialisation of art creates an artificial need within the recipient.[32] They define the standards. Everything is calculated and becomes calculable. Nothing is therefore left to chance.[33] This is partly true for "RTL" since Reality shows are often designed as social experiments. Therefore, their outcomes are characterized by uncertainty.

Furthermore, Adorno argues that culture has become a commodity through interchangeability. [34] This part of his theory becomes true within Reality TV. For example, "Ich bin ein Star – Holt mich hier raus!" verifies this principle very impressive since the challenges are very similar in each season. The variations are minimally and even the presenters act almost the same each time, especially with their jokes. The "Spiegel" writes: "*As Sonja Zietlow says right at the beginning: "The show is the star, theoretically we could take anyone"*.[35] In case of „RTL" it can be seen, that the same TV-formats are repeated at certain time intervals, usually on an annual basis. According to Adorno, this constant persistence and repetition keeps people from thinking independently. He is right with that because some recipients don't recognize the artificial character of these shows. Like Adorno says, cultural contents have the potential to become social rules and they convey to the consumer what is right and wrong. This is true because consumers watch "Big Brother" and shows like this to compare themselves with the displayed characters. People who watch these programs often chase the dream of becoming part of it and this is a key concept of this genre. It conveys the feeling that it is easy to become an actor. According to Adorno, television makes free time becoming a shadowy continuation of labour which leads to the disappearance of the difference between work and leisure time. [36] It is possible to find this concept within Reality TV. The winning teams or members get rewards

---

[32] Bolanos, Paolo A. (2007). P. 27 – 28.
[33] Adorno, Theodor (2000). P. 365.
[34] Apel, Hartmut (1980). P. 53.
[35] Niggemeier, Stefan (2012). Last Access on 2018.11.03.
[36] Adorno, Theodor (1991). P. 168.

for their work, as we can see by means of "Ich bin ein Star – Holt mich hier raus!". If they fail, they come away empty-handed and hungry. Same with "Bauer sucht Frau", which includes the motive of the working farmer. The consumer only watches the actor within his or her working sphere. This creates the feeling, that all time should be structured like working time.[37] Furthermore, the use or utilitarian value of television as learning medium was replaced by exchange or hedonic values. Reality shows offer hedonic value because of their pseudo-reality setting and pseudo-escape from life, whereas their only use-value is an impractical advice for strange situations.

Furthermore, culture industry is in Adornos' sense a betrayal of the masses. Like in "Ich bin ein Star – Holt mich hier raus!", the consumer gets the feeling of being involved in the process of eliminating members of the cast by the act of voting even though he is highly influenced by the image the production team creates by the selection of broadcasted content. Consequently, it is possible to create a completely new image of somebody by showing only certain sections which can falsify the original situation. The true power is owned by the producer.[38] Television thus becomes a piece of reality and its artificial character obscures. Adorno suspects that television makes its viewers fixed and passive in their lives rather than encouraging change or even emancipatory action. In contrary, with reality TV a new form of interactivity evolved. The consumers can become part of the show in two ways, either through physical appearance on the show itself or through voting for or against participating contestants. In addition, the recipient can consume supplementary content on the internet website "RTL Now" if he missed a show. This consumption is rather non-linear than linear which implies a high degree of activity because certain contents must be searched.

---

[37] Potts, Graham (2007). P. 3.
[38] Ibid., P. 4.

Another crucial argument against Adornos thoughts is given by "human need satisfaction" theories. According to gratitude researches, television offers a way to satisfy the audiences' need for emotional involvement, distraction, pastime and belonging. An emotional gratification of needs occurs, where an emotional proximity of audience and television protagonists is achieved.[39] Furthermore, voyeurism, social comparison without self-disclosure and useful advice make these shows attractive. But this social comparison is not only interesting for the lower educated audience but also for intellectuals since it can serve as vehicle for social distinction, boost of ones' self-esteem and strengthening of one's own identity.[40]

Furthermore, these shows include various types of individuals which facilitates the identification aspect. This in turn, offers the ability of creating deeper para-social relationships. Para-social relationships are defined as seeming face-to-face relationships which evolve between the consumer and a mediated person. This can help people to handle their loneliness and fulfilling of the desire for interaction. Reality TV shows are a suitable platform for the aim of building para-social relationships because they show people in a way the recipient can relate to.[41] Even celebrities become approachable through these programs because they show private insights, characteristics and specific habits. The consumer gets deeper information about them than he would through interviews or films because the content of Reality TV is highly related to the actual lives of its participants. This creates intimacy between the contestant and the viewer.[42] On the other hand, this situation makes consumers becoming 'temple slaves' in Adornos' sense because the audience starts worshiping the figures within the shows if the consume becomes too excessive and the risk increases, that the consumer forgets about the one-

[39] Doeveling, Katrin (2008). P. 15.
[40] Prof. Süss, Daniel (2017) as quoted by HD Austria. Last Access on 2018.12.10.
[41] Dyer, Caitlin Elizabeth (2010). P. 3 - 4.
[42] Ibid., P. 7 - 8.

sided nature of this relationship. Furthermore, the event which is broadcasted already occurred and the individuals moved on with their lives outside the gaze of the television.

## 4. Conclusion

Adornos' theory is still an adequate tool for the analysis of the current television environment. The previous discussion shows that in some point, Adornos theory became true in case of Reality TV. Adorno sees the culture industry as a fraud of the masses, as the needs of individuals are manipulated in ways that lack critical thinking skills. This is partly true since a big part of the audience still don't know about the artificiality in form of scripts and constructed situations and consumes them without questioning. The reason is the genres' claim for its relation to reality. This authentic impression covers its artificial character. As Adorno already knew in 1991, everybody is affected by media and television. Therefore, media influences people's thinking and requires critical reception.

But not every thought of Adorno became realized through Reality TV. Adorno and Horkheimers' quote: *"Nevertheless the culture industry remains the entertainment business."*[43] can be applied as reference for the purpose of Reality TV. People watch these shows to satisfy their need for entertainment, curiosity and belonginess. The programs meet the longing for "real" participating in the world of other people through a "media window".[44]

Finally, it would be too simple to regard Reality TV only as stultification and kind of the pejorative term "Trash-TV". None of the temporary television phenomenon can be interpreted only as black or white. Or like Adorno would say:

*"The effect of television cannot be adequately expressed in terms of success or failure, likes or dislikes, approval or dis- approval"*[45]

---

[43] Adorno, Theodor W. / Horkheimer, M. (2002). P. 136.
[44] Neumann-Braun, Klaus (n.d.). Last Access 2018.12.01.
[45] Adorno, Theodor W. (1954). P. 213.

# 5. Sources

Adorno, Theodor W. (1954). How to look at television. In: The quarterly of film radio and television, Vol. 8, No. 3.

Adorno, Theodor W. / Horkheimer, M. (2002). Dialectic of enlightenment. (G. Noeri, Trans.). Stanford University Press.

Adorno, Theodor (2000). Negative Dialektik. Suhrkamp.

Adorno, Theodor (1991). The Culture Industry: Selected Essays on Mass Culture. London, Routledge.

Apel, Hartmut (1980). Die Gesellschaftstheorie der Frankfurter Schule, Materialien zur kritischen Theorie von Adorno, Horkheimer und Marcuse, Verlag Moritz Diesterweg GmbH & Co., Frankfurt am Main.

Behrens, Roger (2003). Adorno-ABC. Reclam, Leipzig.

Bleicher, Joan Kristin (2018). Dein Leben – unser Fernsehen. https://www.tagesspiegel.de/medien/reality-tv-in-deutschland-dein-leben-unser-fernsehen/22755870.html - Last Access on 2018.12.01.

Bolanos, Paolo A. (2007). The critical role of art: Adorno between utopia and dystopia. In: Kritike. Vol. 1, No. 1. P. 25 – 31.

Brown, Patrick (2010). Nobody Wants to Go Home: A Unified Theory of Reality TV. https://themillions.com/2010/01/nobody-wants-to-go-home-a-unified-theory-of-reality-tv.html- Last Access on 2018.12.10.

Chalaby, Jean K. (2011). The making of an entertainment revolution: How the TV format trade became a global industry. In: European Journal of Communication. Vol. 26 issue: 4, P. 293-309.

Doeveling, Katrin (2008). Powered by emotions'. Zur Macht der Emotionen im Reality TV. Klagenfurt.

Dyer, Caitlin Elizabeth (2010). Reality Television: Using Para-social relationship theory and economic theory to define the success of network reality programming. Texas.

Grzeschik, David (2018). <<Bachelor in Paradise>>. http://www.quotenmeter.de/n/101661/quotencheck-bachelor-in-paradise - Last Access on 2018.12.15.

Grzeschik, David (2018). <<Tatort>>, Löwen, Dschungel: Das waren die meistgeschauten TV-Sendungen 2017. http://www.quotenmeter.de/n/98076/tatort-loewen-dschungel-das-waren-die-meistgeschauten-tv-sendungen-2017– Last Access on 2018.10.20.

Köpfe (2018). Dschungelcamp 2018 erntet erneut starke Quoten. http://www.quotenmeter.de/n/98856/dschungelcamp-2018-erntet-erneut-starke-quoten - Last Access on 2018.12-09.

Maeder, Dominik (2018). Economies of Contingency. Lost, Dschungelcamp, and the governmental poetics of being cast away. In: Beil, Benjamin et al. (ed.). Lost in Media. LIT Verlag Münster.

Mark, Andrejevic (2003). Reality TV: The Work of Being Watched. Rowman & Littlefield Publishers, Inc., Maryland.

Meier, Urs (2000). Das Fernsehen kommt zu sich selbst. Kommunikationskultur im Zeichen von „Big Brother". https://www.medienheft.ch/kritik/bibliothek/BigBrother.html - Last Access on 2018.11.20.

Mikos, Lothar (2000). Big Brother als performatives Realityfernsehen – Ein Fernsehformat im Kontext der Entwicklung des Unterhaltungsfernsehens. In: Weber, Frank (ed.). Big Brother: inszenierte Banalität zur Prime Time. LIT Verlag Münster.

Neumann-Braun, Klaus (n.d.). Die Faszination von Reality-TV. https://www.unibas.ch/de/Forschung/Uni-Nova/Uni-Nova-118/Uni-Nova-118-Kolumne.html - Last Access 2018.12.01.

Niemeier, Timo (2012). <<Der Bachelor>>. http://www.quotenmeter.de/cms/?p1=n&p2=55140&p3= - Last Access on 2018.12.07.

Niggemeier, Stefan (2012). Dschungelcamp-Auftakt. Die Erotik des Ekels. http://www.spiegel.de/kultur/tv/dschungelcamp-auftakt-die-erotik-des-ekels-a-809040.html - Last Access on 2018.11.03.

Nöthling, Timo (2018). <<Promi Big Brother>>. http://www.quotenmeter.de/n/103500/quotencheck-promi-big-brother - Last Access on 2018.12.08.

Lehmann, Sophie (2012). Performing emotions: A case study on audience reception of the German docusoap Bauer sucht Frau. Stockholm.

Potts, Graham (2007). Adorno on ‚The Donald': Reality Television as Culture Industry. In: Problematique, Issue 11.

Presseportal (2018). 28,4 Prozent Marktanteil für die Mediengruppe „RTL" Deutschland im September 2018. https://www.presseportal.de/pm/72183/4075913 - Last Access on 2018.11.28.

Prof. Süss, Daniel (2017) as quoted by HD Austria in: Bachelor & Co: Woher kommen die beliebtesten Reality Shows? https://www.hdaustria.at/blog/reality-shows/ - Last Access on 2018.12.10.

„RTL" interactive GmbH (2018). Das „Wer wird Millionär? – Prominenten-Special" mit Günther Jauch bei TV NOW online nachholen. https://www."RTL".de/cms/das-wer-wird-millionaer-prominenten-special-mit-guenther-jauch-bei-tv-now-online-nachholen-2713297.html - Last Access on 2018.12.12.

Sallhoff, Daniel (2017). <<Bauer sucht Frau>> trotz Verlusten weiter an der Spitze. http://www.quotenmeter.de/n/96798/bauer-sucht-frau-trotz-verlusten-weiter-an-der-spitze - Last Access on 2018.12.05.

Seier, Andrea (2014). Subjektivität, Körper, Technologien: Der soziale Flow des Fernsehens. LIT Verlag, Münster.

Stern (2017). Diese Trash-TV-Formate finden Deutsche am primitivsten. https://www.stern.de/kultur/tv/tv-trashformate--die-sendungen-finden-deutsche-am-primitivsten-7430338.html - Last Access on 2018.12.01.

Stern (2018). Diese Sender stehen im schlechten Ruf. https://www.stern.de/kultur/tv/trash-tv--diese-sender-stehen-im-schlechten-ruf-7852666.html - Last Access on 2018.12.10.

Stubenböck, Julia (2014). Erzählstrategien im Reality-TV. Wie „RTL" & Co uns Geschichten erzählen. Diplomica Verlag GmbH, Hamburg.

Welt (n.d.). Die 20 beliebtesten TV-Sendungen der Deutschen. https://www.welt.de/fernsehen/gallery13416799/Die-20-beliebtesten-TV-Sendungen-der-Deutschen.html - Last Access on 2018.11.20.

Zeitungsverlag tz München GmbH & Co. KG (2018). Gagen im Dschungelcamp: Diese Kandidatin bekommt am meisten. https://www.tz.de/tv/dschungelcamp-2018-gagen-dschungel-kandidaten-zr-7175479.html - Last Access on 2018.11.06.